How To Use Augmentative and Alternative Communication

PRO-ED Series on Autism Spectrum Disorders

Edited by Richard L. Simpson

Titles in the Series

How To Develop and Implement Visual Supports

How To Do Discrete Trial Training

How To Do Incidental Teaching

How To Plan a Structured Classroom

How To Support Children with Problem Behavior

How To Teach Social Skills and Plan for Peer Social Interactions

How To Use Augmentative and Alternative Communication

How To Use Joint Action Routines

How To Use Video Modeling

How To Write and Implement Social Scripts

PRO-ED Series on Autism Spectrum Disorders

How To Use Augmentative and Alternative Communication

Billy T. Ogletree

Thomas Oren

pro·ed
An International Publisher

8700 Shoal Creek Boulevard
Austin, Texas 78757-6897
800/897-3202   Fax 800/397-7633
www.proedinc.com

© 2006 by PRO-ED, Inc.
8700 Shoal Creek Boulevard
Austin, Texas 78757-6897
800/897-3202   Fax 800/397-7633
www.proedinc.com

Library of Congress Cataloging-in-Publication Data

Ogletree, Billy T.
   How to use augmentative and alternative communication / Billy T. Ogletree and Thomas Oren.
      p. cm. — (PRO-ED series on autism spectrum disorders)
   Includes bibliographical references.
   ISBN 1-4164-0150-4 (soft cover : alk. paper)
   1. Autism—Patients—Language.   2. Autism—Patients—Rehabilitation.
3. Communication devices for people with disabilities.   I. Oren, Thomas.
II. Title.   III. Series.

RC553.A88045 2006
616.85'882—dc22

                                                                      2005015227

Art Director: Jason Crosier
Designer: Nancy McKinney-Point
This book is designed in Nexus Serif TF and Neutra Text.

Printed in the United States of America

2 3 4 5 6 7 8 9 10 11   16 15 14 13 12

Contents

From the Editor

About Autism Spectrum Disorders

Autism spectrum disorders (ASD) are complex, neurologically based developmental disabilities that typically appear early in life. The Autism Society of America (2004) estimates that as many as 1.5 million people in the United States have autism or some form of pervasive developmental disorder. Indeed, its prevalence makes ASD an increasingly common and currently the fastest growing developmental disability. ASD are perplexing and enigmatic. According to the *Diagnostic and Statistical Manual of Mental Disorders,* individuals with ASD have difficulty in interacting normally with others; exhibit speech, language, and communication difficulties (e.g., delayed speech, echolalia); insist on routines and environmental uniformity; engage in self-stimulatory and stereotypic behaviors; and respond atypically to sensory stimuli (American Psychiatric Association, 2000; Simpson & Myles, 1998). In some cases, aggressive and self-injurious behavior may be present in these individuals. Yet, in tandem with these characteristics, children with ASD often have normal patterns of physical growth and development, a wide range of cognitive and language capabilities, and some individuals with ASD have highly developed and unique abilities (Klin, Volkmar, & Sparrow, 2000). These widely varied characteristics necessitate specially designed interventions and strategies orchestrated by knowledgeable and skilled professionals.

Preface to the Series

Teaching and managing learners with ASD can be demanding, but favorable outcomes for children and youth with autism and autism-related disabilities depend on professionals using appropriate and valid methods in their education. Because identifying and correctly using effective teaching methods is often enormously challenging (National Research Council, 2001; Simpson et al., 2005), it is the intent of this series to provide professionals with scientifically based methods for intervention. Each book in the series is designed to assist professionals and parents in choosing and correctly using a variety of interventions that have the potential to produce significant benefits for children and youth with ASD. Written in a user-friendly, straightforward fashion by qualified and experienced professionals, the books are aimed at individuals who seek practical solutions and strategies for successfully working with learners with ASD.

Richard L. Simpson
Series Editor

References

American Psychiatric Association. (2000). *Diagnostic and statistical manual of mental disorders* (4th ed., text rev.). Washington, DC: Author.

Autism Society of America. (2004). *What is autism?* Retrieved March 11, 2005, from http://autism-society.org

Klin, A., Volkmar, F., & Sparrow, S. (2000). *Asperger syndrome.* New York: Guilford Press.

National Research Council. (2001). *Educating children with autism.* Committee on Educational Interventions for Children with Autism, Division of Behavioral and Social Sciences and Education. Washington, DC: National Academy Press.

Simpson, R., de Boer-Ott, S., Griswold, D., Myles, B., Byrd, S., Ganz, J., et al. (2005). *Autism spectrum disorders: Interventions and treatments for children and youth.* Thousand Oaks, CA: Corwin Press.

Simpson, R. L., & Myles, B. S. (1998). *Educating children and youth with autism: Strategies for effective practice.* Austin, TX: PRO-ED.

Introduction

There are myriad challenges facing those who serve individuals with autism spectrum disorders (ASD). These often relate, either directly or indirectly, to communication impairment. For decades, researchers have worked to develop treatments that facilitate communication success. Efforts have yielded preventative, remedial, and compensatory methodologies (Wilcox, 1987). Preventative treatments use aggressive prenatal care, comprehensive nutrition programs, and early intervention to minimize the likelihood of communication impairment before it occurs. In contrast, remedial treatments address existing communication deficits through hands-on and consultative interventions of varied directiveness. Finally, compensatory treatments promote effective communication through means other than natural speech. The practice of using compensatory treatments to supplement or replace natural speech and writing is referred to as Augmentative and Alternative Communication (AAC).

This manual reviews AAC applications for individuals with ASD. In the section titled Overview of AAC and ASD, AAC is defined and described to provide the knowledge necessary for effective clinical decision making. Basic facts are overviewed and the impact of AAC on the emergence of natural speech is discussed. In addition, the communicative impairments of persons with ASD are briefly reviewed and the characteristics of ASD that make AAC a logical choice for so many individuals are considered. This section ends with a review of literature specific to AAC use among persons with ASD. The following section, Promoting Effective Practices, presents a series of recommended practices to help guide parents and practitioners in the establishment and implementation of AAC. The section titled Juan's AAC Story illustrates recommended practices through scenarios from the life of one individual. Throughout this manual there are exercises and questions designed to encourage the reader to apply content in real-world ways. Clearly, this work is not an exhaustive resource. It is, however, a starting point and guide for those interested in using AAC with children and adults with ASD.

Overview of AAC and ASD

AAC Facts

What Is AAC?

Lloyd, Fuller, and Arvidson (1997) define AAC as both a process and a discipline. These authors suggest that the process of AAC involves "the supplementation or replacement of natural speech and/or writing" (p. 1). As a discipline, Lloyd et al. note that AAC is a field using "a variety of symbols, strategies, and techniques to assist people who are unable to meet their communication needs through natural speech and/or writing" (p. 1).

Who Uses and Provides AAC?

Recipients of AAC services are typically individuals who are not proficient oral or written communicators. This group includes persons with congenital and acquired impairments including, but not limited to, mental retardation, cerebral palsy, autism, developmental apraxia, amyotrophic lateral sclerosis (ALS), traumatic brain injury, stroke, and spinal cord injury. Beukelman and Ansel (1995) estimate that 8 to 12 persons per 1,000 present severe expressive communication deficits and could benefit from AAC.

AAC, as a discipline, is typically practiced by inter- or transdisciplinary teams. Members of interdisciplinary teams function interdependently and collaboratively while maintaining their professional roles (Ogletree, 1999). Transdisciplinary teams also value interdependence and collaboration, yet their members practice joint service delivery and professional role release (Lyon & Lyon, 1980). Both of these team structures include parents and family members as equal partners in decision making.

In addition to family members, AAC teams include, but are not limited to, speech–language pathologists, audiologists, occupational therapists, physical therapists, special educators, general education teachers, assistive technology specialists, social workers, nurses, vision specialists, psychologists, and rehabilitation engineers (Dalton Moffitt, 1999). Dalton Moffitt (1999) notes that AAC teams may consist of a small core group of disciplines (e.g., the speech–language pathologist, special educator, general education teacher, and occupational therapist) that consult with other allied health colleagues as needed. Often the speech–language pathologist will serve in a leadership role for AAC teams specific to the organization and implementation of services.

What Are Specific AAC Services?

AAC services include evaluation, feature matching and trial intervention, device or system procurement, implementation, and follow-up. Figure 1 illustrates how these services can be viewed as a circular process leading to improved communication for users and their communicative partners.

Evaluation includes examination of the user, his or her environments, and the devices or systems used to meet user needs. Beukelman and Mirenda (1998) note that AAC evaluations should address current and, when possible, future needs. User evaluations should review physical competence (e.g., vision, hearing, positioning, seating), access to systems or devices (e.g., the ability to move in a way that allows for direct or alternative access), cognitive functioning, and communication and language abilities. Communication and language evaluations must address existing expressive and receptive

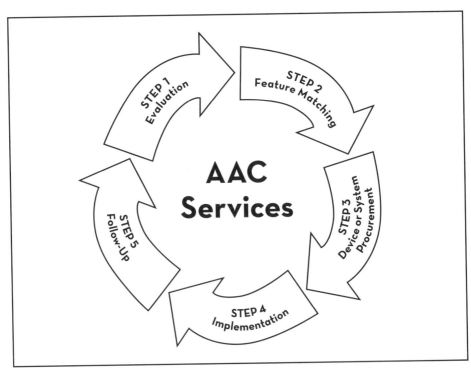

FIGURE 1. The circular process of AAC services.

abilities as well as signal and symbol preferences, vocabulary choices, voice output, and writing applications. Specific to signals and symbols, decisions have to be made regarding unaided (i.e., signals or symbols that do not require materials external to the individual—sounds, expressions, gestures, or signs) or aided (i.e., symbols that are external to the user—photos, boards, devices, computers) options. A discussion of unaided and aided AAC specific to individuals with ASD is provided later in this section.

Environments need to be evaluated to determine both the opportunities and challenges they present. Beukelman and Mirenda (1998) note that environments may present a host of barriers to successful AAC use. These include policy barriers (e.g., the segregation of students preventing interactions with nondisabled peers), practice barriers (e.g., the practice of not allowing devices to leave school grounds), attitude barriers (e.g., an individual's personal beliefs that might limit student participation independent of policies and practices), knowledge barriers (e.g., an individual's lack of information needed to operate a system or device), and skill barriers (e.g., a supporting individual's limited success with a device in the presence of adequate knowledge).

As an extension of evaluation, devices or systems must be assessed to determine what best fits users' needs. This process has been referred to as feature matching (Costello & Shane, 1994; Glennen, 1997). This final step of the team evaluation allows team members to match critical features of devices or systems with user needs to generate a list of possible AAC solutions. This list typically is used to generate one or more trial runs where devices or systems may be borrowed and used temporarily. Trial interventions generally lead to specific procurement decisions.

Device or system procurement efforts are obviously limited to aided AAC options. This process is often led by a representative of the AAC team who is familiar with vendors and knowledgeable about local and national funding processes. Parents and family members, constituency representatives (e.g., from schools and community facilities), and area agency representatives (e.g., from Vocational Rehabilitation) assist in the procurement process by contributing ideas and offering resources. AAC funding is typically the direct result of collaborative partnerships formed between most or all of the parties mentioned previously.

Procuring an AAC device or system may require several applications to funding sources. To increase the likelihood of funding success, Beukelman and Mirenda (1998) suggest a multistep process. They recommend beginning with a survey of possible sources available for use. These sources may fund various AAC activities (e.g., evaluation, purchase). Beukelman and Mirenda suggest that once a survey is completed, an individualized funding plan tying funding sources to specific AAC activities should be generated. This plan serves as the funding blueprint for the team member assigned to pursue funding options. If applications are denied, appeals can be filed and new sources can be identified.

AAC devices or systems are typically introduced by a speech–language pathologist who may be assisted, as needed, by other team members. Oftentimes, implementation is directed by professionals uninvolved in the evaluation process. This can result in treatment disruptions if intervention plans are not clearly identified by the evaluating team. An ideal solution is to assign evaluating team members a transitional role in the establishment of AAC treatment plans. Although this protracts the evaluation process, it provides continuity and increases the probability of success.

Initial AAC implementation may involve a period of direct services with the speech–language pathologist, where the user becomes familiar with his or her device or system. This will be followed by, or occur concurrently with, efforts to create daily applications for the device or system. The speech–language pathologist will probably identify other individuals in the user's life (e.g., teachers, family members, co-workers) to assist with this process. Together, this group will address everyday issues like environmental barriers, technology breakdowns, changing vocabulary needs, and access limitations. Eventually, the speech–language pathologist will provide more of a support role for the user and his or her communicative partners. As the user's needs change, the speech–language pathologist may need to once again assume a more direct role in providing ongoing services.

AAC implementations rarely end. This is particularly true for individuals with more severe disabilities. Follow-up is simply the speech–language pathologist's or AAC team member's way of assuring an appropriate level of support for individuals who have cycled through the initial evaluation and implementation process. Follow-ups may occur at regularly scheduled intervals or be conducted more informally as observations or interviews. The intent is to determine the effectiveness of prescribed devices or systems specific to the user's immediate and future needs.

Does AAC Impede the Speech Process for Users?

Before moving to information specific to AAC application for individuals with ASD, one frequently asked question must be addressed. Understandably, many parents and communicative partners are reluctant to support the use of AAC with their child, student, or peer due to the belief that communication via AAC may, in some way, impede the acquisition of natural speech. Several research studies have indirectly addressed this question. Findings have suggested that individuals exposed to AAC have experienced increased vocal imitation skills (Carr & Dores, 1981; Clarke, Remington, & Light, 1988; Schepis et al., 1982) and improved or maintained abilities in natural speech (Clarke et al., 1988). These reports support the tentative conclusion that the introduction of AAC will probably not prevent speech development and may actually facilitate it.

EXERCISES

After learning a little about AAC, do you think that there are individuals who are too severely impaired to benefit from AAC services?

Why are AAC services described as a circular process?

In the first exercise question, you were correct if you answered that there are no prerequisites for AAC use, even among individuals who are severely impaired. For years, professionals in the field of AAC have worked to discourage the notion of prerequisites. The bottom line is that all persons should have access to communication options regardless of the severity or nature of their handicapping conditions. This position is supported by the National Joint Committee for the Communication Needs of Persons with Severe Disabilities (McCarthy et al., 1998). You may be thinking, "What if individuals cannot communicate intentionally (i.e., purposefully)?" Our response is that systems and devices can be introduced with nonintentional communicators. This group, however, may require a greater degree of partner support (i.e., partial participation) and interpretation to experience communicative success through AAC.

To answer the second exercise question, the process of AAC is circular in that it is ongoing. The five AAC services described previously build on each other. That is, evaluation leads to trial runs and procurement, which leads to implementation and follow-up. Likewise, new needs of an individual in follow-up can reinitiate evaluation services and the circular nature of the AAC process.

ASD and Communication Impairment

What follows is a review of the communicative abilities of persons with ASD. Both expressive abilities and comprehension are discussed.

Expressive Abilities

Ogletree (in press) subdivides persons with ASD into three groups, according to their communicative abilities. He refers to one group as nonverbal communicators. These individuals all communicate without speech, and some are limited to the use of nonsymbolic communication. Nonsymbolic communication is expressed through signals rather than symbols. Examples of signals used by persons with ASD include hand-over-hand "leading" gestures, reaches, vocalizations, and facial expressions. These types of behaviors require context for interpretation. That is, if someone reaches, we interpret their reach as a request based upon our shared awareness of the object in their line of regard. Without the object (i.e., the context), their reaching would not convey a clear meaning.

It should be noted that individuals with ASD use gestural signals less frequently and in a less sophisticated manner than their peers without disabilities (Buitelaar, van Engeland, de Koegal, de Vries, & Van Hoof, 1991). Furthermore, many conventional gestures such as waves and points are largely absent altogether in this population (Wetherby, Prizant, & Hutchinson, 1998). Finally, the vocal signals of persons with ASD have been favorably compared to children with developmental delays in terms of consonant usage; however, children with ASD produce more atypical vocalizations such as screams and yells (Sheinkopf, Mundy, Oller, & Steffens, 2000).

According to Ogletree (in press), nonverbal communicators with ASD may also use simple symbol forms to communicate. Some may be signers, whereas others may express themselves using objects, photographs, or line drawings. It is important to note that nonverbal symbol users, like their nonsymbolic peers, do not use speech.

The communicative behaviors of nonverbal individuals with ASD are typically used to regulate others (i.e., behavior regulation). As communication partners, we interpret these behaviors as requests and protests. For example, a nonsymbolic child with ASD may take your hand (i.e., a leading behavior) and place it on the refrigerator door to convey a request for food. Wetherby (1986) noted that, when individuals with ASD communicate for reasons other than regulating behavior, they typically express social functions first (e.g., greetings) and occasionally communicate to reference joint attention (e.g., commenting). The use of communication to comment, though atypical of this population, is a good prognostic indicator for future communication and language development when present.

The second group described by Ogletree (in press) communicates via emergent verbal abilities. Ogletree notes that emergent verbal communicators use echolalia and some productive speech to express themselves. It is hypothesized that this group's dependence upon gestalt (i.e., holistic) processing contributes to their frequent use of echo. The echolalia used by emergent communicators can be immediate (i.e., occur immediately after a partner's speech), delayed (i.e., follow a partner's speech after a lapsed period of time), or mitigated (i.e., have imitated and generative qualities). The presence of echo is generally thought of as a good prognostic indicator for generative speech development.

The third group described by Ogletree (in press) communicates with speech. Their articulatory or phonologic capabilities are relative strengths, whereas their voice quality often reflects problems with pitch, volume, timing, and stress. These vocal differences can contribute to speech that is staid and invariant (Baltaxe & Simmons, 1977).

This group of productive speech and language users have varying abilities across Bloom and Lahey's (1978) language parameters of form (i.e., morphology and syntax), content (i.e., semantics), and use (i.e., pragmatics). Although the form or structure of this group's language can appear relatively intact (contributing to a perception of language competence), their language content and use can be significantly impaired.

Some of the more prevalent errors with language content observed from persons with ASD include problems with encoding meaning relevant to conversation, literal interpretations, and semantic confusion specific to temporal sequencing (Brook & Bowler, 1992). Reported problems with language use involve impaired paralinguistic or extralinguistic aspects of communication (e.g., the invariant speech patterns mentioned previously), deficits with encoding linguistic intent (e.g., ongoing message evaluation and modification), and compromised social competence (e.g., the ability to establish a topic, take turns in conversation, use gaze; Koegel, 1995).

All three types of communicators described by Ogletree (in press) may express themselves through excess behavior. Doss and Reichle (1991) described excess behavior as "behavior ... that results in self-injury or injury of others, causes damage to the physical environment, interferes with the acquisition of new skills, and/or socially isolates the learner" (p. 215). In persons with ASD and other disabilities, excess behavior may be used to gain attention, request, escape undesirable activities, and protest (Carr & Durand, 1985; Durand & Carr, 1987). The authors of this manual have worked with children and adults who bite, throw objects, flap, ruminate, hit, and pinch to interact with others. Clearly, these types of behaviors can bring negative attention to and isolate the individual with ASD.

Comprehension

Ogletree (in press) notes that comprehension is a developmental process that begins in infancy and continues into adulthood. Initially, infants and toddlers understand their communicative partners through emotion and context. For example, a mother says "No" as her 7-month-old reaches for an electric outlet. The same mother may point to a book as she tells her 19-month-old to "Get me the book." In both instances, meaning is conveyed as much by how and where things are said, as by what is said. As children approach the third year of life, they begin to understand word order. For example, a 30-month-old child would likely respond correctly to a nonsensical play request to "Make that book push the car." Here, meaning is determined by the verbal message rather than the context. As children grow to adulthood, comprehension continues to develop. Vocabularies expand, meaning expressed through complex grammatical structures is mastered, and the often unspoken rules of interaction are understood and applied (e.g., you communicate differently on a playground than in a church).

Comprehension in individuals with ASD is not completely understood. Ogletree (in press) notes that nonverbal communicators with ASD may fail to grasp spoken messages due to their inability to decode the affect and emotion critical to early meaning. These individuals may also miss comprehension cues due to certain learning characteristics common to ASD (e.g., preferences for static stimuli and stimulus over-selectivity; see next section).

The comprehension of emergent verbal communicators has been investigated with respect to its relationship to echolalia. Initially, researchers suspected that comprehension deficits caused echolalia (Stengel, 1964). This perspective changed as theorists proposed a developmental role for echolalia in language emergence for individuals with ASD (Fay, 1969; Howlin, 1982; Rutter & Lockyer, 1967). Today, echolalia is viewed more positively as a bridge to productive language use. Furthermore, echoic utterances have been reported to decrease as comprehension and expressive language abilities become increasingly complex (Roberts, 1989).

For individuals with ASD who use speech, comprehension deficits relate broadly to conversational competence, and more specifically, to impaired expressive language abilities. The conversational competence of this population can be compromised by the neglect of subtle partner cues. For example, failing to recognize and interpret a confused facial expression can lead to missed opportunities to provide needed conversational repair. Twachman-Cullen (2000) suggested that impaired comprehension is an underlying cause of specific expressive deficits observed from individuals with ASD (e.g., errors resulting from literalness, metaphorical language, and perspective taking). This perspective is based on the idea that flexible communication and language expression is dependent upon competent comprehension.

In summary, the communicative abilities of persons with ASD are quite varied. Some individuals may be limited to nonsymbolic or aberrant communicative forms to express themselves. Others may exhibit advanced verbal abilities with relatively subtle social and conversational deficits. Regardless of the level of their expressive abilities, individuals with ASD can be expected to demonstrate some impairments in comprehension that limit their communicative competence.

EXERCISES

Write a description of the communication abilities of someone diagnosed with ASD you know or have worked with. In which of Ogletree's (in press) three communicator categories does he or she best fit?

Why is echolalia presently considered a positive indicator of continued speech and language development in individuals with ASD?

The answer to the first exercise question depends on the communicative characteristics you listed. If you described an individual that exclusively communicates via gestures, vocal behaviors, facial expressions, and two- or three-dimensional symbols, you are probably referring to Ogletree's (in press) category of nonverbal communicators. If your description included echolalia or simple productive speech, your example fits the emergent verbal category. Of course, if your example was an individual who is verbal, yet has social and conversational limitations, you are probably describing a productive speech and language user.

The second exercise question asked why echolalia is presently considered to be a positive indicator for speech and language development in individuals with ASD. The answer relates to the current conceptualization of language emergence in this population. Persons with ASD are thought to use gestalt language processing or language chunking. This allows them to go from being nonverbal to using short echolalic phrases. These phrases, though seemingly complex, probably represent the equivalent of one word for the user. They are, in essence, a chunked piece of language. As individuals using echo continue to develop speech and language, they learn to break down their chunks into productive meaningful speech.

What Makes AAC a Reasonable Fit for Many Persons with ASD?

As was described previously, individuals with ASD have significant communication, speech, or language deficits. Accordingly, they may need assistance with basic communication and can frequently benefit from the introduction of AAC. Many learning characteristics observed in persons with ASD make AAC a particularly good communication intervention choice for this population. These traits are reviewed next and are discussed with respect to how they impact AAC learning and use.

Schuler (1995) noted three distinct learning characteristics related to ASD including (a) a deficit with information processing rooted in deficient coding and categorization abilities, (b) a preference for static rather than transient stimuli, and (c) a tendency to be drawn to a single stimulus component (e.g., stimulus overselectivity). In addition, persons with ASD have been reported to show a clear preference for visual learning (Schuler & Baldwin, 1981) and the occasional presence of hyperlexia (Cobrinik, 1974, 1982). It is easy to reason that an individual with these needs and strengths would learn most efficiently if stimuli were organized, redundant, salient, visual, and static. It is interesting to note that these stimulus qualities pervade AAC interventions.

Organization and Redundancy

Whether aiding communication input or output, effective AAC use relies upon organization and redundancy. As for organization, symbols are typically chosen and arranged in a structure that facilitates their use. This might include color coding or placement according to word class, categories, or frequency of use. These simple organizational strategies can promote rapid and successful symbol selection. As another organizational strategy, messages can be encoded or decoded according to logical patterns. For example, the message "Good morning" can be encoded on a device using a Qwerty or alphabet keyboard under the letters "GM." This type of encoding encourages access speed while reducing user effort (i.e., you select fewer keys to form your message). Finally, many voice output communication aids (VOCA) use prediction strategies as a means of organizing and facilitating message delivery. An example of prediction would be when the selection of one symbol on a VOCA causes other related symbols to light up, reducing the searching required to create a multisymbol message. In AAC, message redundancy is evident with respect to the multimodal use of auditory, visual, and orthographic symbols. For example, many AAC systems provide to users numerous symbol forms to promote communication success. A user may sign a request and select a requesting symbol from an array of line drawings. Likewise, a partner may ask a question of a user while redundantly augmenting his or her input by gesturing, signing, or touching an appropriate symbol.

Clearly, the organization and redundancy inherent in AAC can be one answer for the deficient information processing abilities of individuals with ASD. First, it seems reasonable to assume that the consistent organization of symbols in AAC could assist users with symbol learning and, in turn, expressive abilities. Furthermore, one can speculate that the message input of partners without disabilities could be greatly enhanced through the symbol and message redundancy evident in AAC. For example, a partner's selection of a question mark symbol on a communication board while asking a question, or signing a word while saying the word, may assist the understanding and ultimate communicative success of a child with ASD.

Symbol and Message Saliency

Finally, symbol saliency is a critical element of AAC interventions for most individuals with ASD. Saliency, in this case, involves both a symbol's clarity or recognition value and its meaningfulness to the user. The transient and arbitrary nature of natural speech may limit its effectiveness with persons with autism, especially with respect to message comprehension. In contrast, AAC symbols like objects, photographs, line drawings, and print can be generated so that they are very clear representations of meaningful referents in a user's environment.

Clearly, AAC seems to address many of the learning needs and preferences of persons with ASD. This section ends with a review of AAC options (including systems and approaches) typically used by this population. Although this review is not exhaustive, it provides an overview of AAC use among persons with ASD and serves as a segue to the next section's discussion of recommended practices.

Visual and Static Symbols

A person using AAC typically uses static visual symbols. From physical two-dimensional objects to photographs, line drawings, print, signs, and gestures, many AAC symbols have a static and visual quality. Even the transient nature of digitized or synthesized speech is typically paired with static visual symbols in AAC systems. The presence of static visual symbols provides the AAC user with increased processing time and, potentially, improved symbol comprehension and use.

Print used in conjunction with static symbols increases message redundancy while playing to a potential strength of persons with ASD (i.e., hyperlexia). Cobrinik (1974, 1982) noted that hyperlexia appears in children with a wide range of disabilities but most often occurs in those with autism. Silberberg and Silberberg (1967) reported that characteristics of hyperlexia include reading levels that exceed cognitive and language abilities and the compulsive or indiscriminant reading of words. These abilities occur early and in the absence of specific instruction. Children who are hyperlexic typically do not show comprehension abilities consistent with their expressive reading levels.

Obviously, individuals with ASD who are hyperlexic would likely be more expressive if presented with print in conjunction with graphic symbols. This increased expressiveness could draw positive attention to their perceived communication abilities and promote increased interaction with partners. Hyperlexic abilities may also aid the message comprehension of users with ASD. For example, a partner who makes a request while pointing to a printed word expressing that request may experience greater success conveying his or her message.

AAC and Individuals with ASD

This review of AAC and individuals with ASD includes both unaided and aided AAC options. Unaided AAC requires nothing external to the communicator. Examples include gesture systems, sign language, vocalizations, and facial expressions. In contrast, aided AAC requires external communication components. Object or picture boards, picture rings, VOCAs, and computerized devices are all examples of aided communication.

Unaided Options

Mirenda and Erickson (2000) note that natural gestures and vocalizations are a good starting point for interventions for many individuals with ASD. This is particularly true for persons showing little interest in intentional communication. It should be noted that gestures are the predominant communication form used by many nonverbal individuals with ASD (Wetherby, Yonclas, & Bryan, 1989). Accordingly, the promotion of gestures as an unaided AAC choice would seem prudent. McLean, Brady, McLean, and Behrens (1999) suggested that individuals with more severe disabilities who use gestures involving contact with objects or people could benefit from intervention to encourage more distal gestural forms (e.g., points without contact). These authors note that distal gestures may be a step toward eventual symbol use.

A common mistake made by interventionists serving the nonsymbolic communicator with ASD is the introduction of symbolic communication prior to the establishment of the basic elements of communication (e.g., turn taking and joint attention; Mirenda, 2000). Working with gestural forms within predictable routine formats allows for a focus on these more basic skills central to effective symbol use.

Sign language served as the early form of unaided symbolic intervention for persons with ASD. In the 1970s, numerous studies demonstrated the efficacy of sign use (Fulwiler & Fouts, 1976; Webster, McPherson, Sloman, Evans, & Kuchar, 1973), and signing was considered very promising as an intervention option. By the 1980s, isolated signing gave way to total communication (i.e., signing and speaking) as a recommended practice for persons with more severe disabilities, including autism (Bryen & Joyce, 1985). Total communication emphasized joint communication through signing and speech and was thought to promote communicative effectiveness by increasing message redundancy.

Obviously, the use of signing with persons with ASD presents some limitations. First, it is likely that many individuals in the user's environment will not be signers. This effectively reduces the number of communicative partners for the signing individual. Second, many persons with ASD produce signs that are inconsistent with established forms expected by the signing community. Idiosyncratic signing requires that partners know not only signs, but also how users' signs differ from standard production. A lack of familiarity with users' signs can further reduce the effectiveness of signing for persons with ASD. Third, even though signs have a more static production quality than speech, they are still transient when compared to aided graphic symbol forms. As discussed earlier, static symbols appear to be preferred by persons with ASD.

Aided Options

The following discussion of aided communication options is organized according to system sophistication. Simple displays of graphic and orthographic symbols are reviewed first, followed by a more limited review of aided applications involving VOCAs and computer hard- and software. Each section includes a review of some research findings and a discussion of practical applications.

Since the early days of AAC, simple arrays of graphic symbols have been used to promote the communicative success (communication and language comprehension and production) of persons with ASD. The following discussion considers simple aided AAC applications. Aided input is considered first, followed by aided output. Approaches that emphasize input and output are highlighted.

Numerous authors have recommended graphic symbols (e.g., objects, photographs, line drawings, print) as a means to augment communication and language input (Hodgdon, 1995; Quill, 1995). For example, a communicative partner may touch relevant symbols on a user's symbol board as he or she asks questions or provides choices. Augmented input can assist persons with ASD with task completion and transitions within and between tasks. Objects, photographs, line drawings, or print (these could be used in combination) may be used to create a schedule of daily events or an illustration of steps to be completed in a single event. In this example, partners would convey the activities of the day or the steps to a work sequence by directing the individual to his or her schedule.

Some authors have cautioned those working with persons with ASD not to provide input through too many simultaneous communication modalities (Sigafoos, Drasgow, & Schlosser, 2003). Their concern stems from this population's tendency to selectively respond to stimuli (see learning characteristics discussed earlier in this section). Stimulus overselectivity can contribute to undue attention to one input modality or stimulus and neglect of another. Obviously, this could affect both input and output and should be a consideration in AAC assessment and intervention.

Persons with ASD also frequently use graphic symbols to express themselves. Again, objects (whole or partial), photographs, line drawings, and print can be used in isolation or in combination. These symbols can be arrayed, among other ways, on boards, in wallets, on symbol rings, or in notebooks. Typically, symbols are organized according to themes or categories (e.g., people, activities, favorite foods), parts of speech (nouns, verbs, objects), or by use patterns (e.g., frequency of use). Graphic symbols can also be used individually. For example, single symbols can be exchanged for desired objects or activities.

Symbol exchange as a means of communication has been pursued by Frost and Bondy (2002), developers of the *Picture Exchange Communication System* (PECS). PECS is a training approach that has been particularly successful with persons with ASD. It teaches users to initiate communicative acts in pursuit of concrete outcomes. The approach is based on the belief that communication is a social exchange. Users are initially taught to exchange symbols for objects with little regard for the symbols themselves. Training focuses on the symbol exchange as a means to an end. As the learner successfully begins to exchange symbols, emphasis can be shifted to symbol differentiation. Weitz, Dexter, and Moore (1997) note that PECS is an excellent training alternative for individuals beginning to exhibit intentional communication. They also suggest that PECS can lead to more sophisticated AAC applications.

Thus far, simple aided AAC applications have been considered individually with respect to input and output augmentation. Some programs have been developed that target both of these outcomes. For example, Aided Language Stimulation (ALS) was introduced by Goossens (1989) as a receptive and expressive teaching strategy. ALS is based on the observation that a user's competence with AAC systems is, in large part, dependent on the partner's use of the system with him or her. Accordingly, partners serve as facilitators, selecting symbols from the user's symbol array to support their own interaction. In addition, facilitators use communication systems to respond contingently to users in ways that scaffold (e.g., recast, expand) more advanced communication and language.

A similar program emphasizing augmented input and output is the System for Augmenting Language (SAL). This approach uses VOCAs and will be reviewed later in this section.

In summary, Glennen and DeCoste (1997) noted that the successful use of simple aided AAC options for this population depends on a complete understanding of users' existing nonsymbolic and symbolic communicative forms. This of course necessitates a thorough assessment process. Furthermore, these authors encourage partners and practitioners to be knowledgeable about users' learning styles and preferences. These factors can have a critical impact on symbol selection and use. Finally, Glennen and DeCoste report that decision makers (AAC team members including family members) must take into account users' needs in multiple environments. Communicative needs drive many decisions specific to the construction and use of simple aided systems for this population.

As mentioned previously in this review, VOCAs are portable devices that provide digitized or synthesized speech output. Digitized speech is simply recorded human speech. In contrast, synthesized speech is speech produced with a synthesizer. Although digitized speech will be more intelligible, it can require more device memory and will not be as generative as synthesized speech (i.e., synthesized speech is more flexible in terms of the production of novel utterances). Research specific to VOCA use with persons with ASD is limited. Findings about augmented input and output with VOCAs are reviewed next.

Romski and colleagues (Adamson, Romski, Diffebach, & Sevcik, 1992; Romski & Sevcik, 1996) used VOCAs with persons with developmental disabilities including autism as a means of promoting language comprehension and expression. Their SAL program was very similar to the ALS program reviewed previously. Mirenda (2001) noted two differences between ALS and SAL, including the use of VOCAs and the simplification of elicitation procedures in SAL. Mirenda described the SAL program as follows: "Communication displays using visual-graphic symbols with a printed word gloss are constructed for each learner's VOCA, and communication partners are taught to use the symbols plus VOCA to augment their speech input during naturally-occurring communication interactions. Learners are encouraged, though not required, to use the device throughout the day. Like ALS, the SAL relies heavily on partner cooperation and the use of the technique on an ongoing basis in natural settings" (p. 149).

Research findings with SAL are impressive. Adamson et al. (1992) noted that subjects increased their use of symbol forms (e.g., referential symbols such as labels and regulatory symbols like "more") while exposed to SAL. Furthermore, over half of Adamson et al.'s subjects ($n = 13$) developed more sophisticated communicative abilities while using SAL (e.g., combining symbols).

Further research using VOCAs with persons with ASD is limited. In a review of peer-reviewed journals and book chapters specific to AAC applications in autism, Mirenda (2001) found only three related studies. Findings reported potential benefits in two areas: behavior replacement (i.e., replacing excess behavior with voice output messages) and the promotion of natural interpersonal interactions.

Mirenda's (2001) review also addressed the potential benefits of computerized instruction for individuals with ASD. Although few published studies exist, general conclusions can be drawn. First, the use of computers with this population may increase peer interaction, motivation, and communication. Mirenda noted that this observation is primarily supported by anecdotal and observational evidence. Second, computer applications, including software, can facilitate reading, phonological awareness, and verbal behavior. Third, computers with synthesized voice output have been shown to promote spontaneous verbal utterances. Again, these observations are tenuous given the lack of published studies to date.

15

In conclusion, providers have many unaided and aided AAC options available as they consider appropriate augmentation for persons with ASD. For individuals with more limited abilities, gestural forms may be preferable. For those who are symbolic, graphic symbols with or without voice output may be deemed appropriate. Finally, some students may also enjoy specific learning and communication benefits from exposure to computers with and without voice output.

EXERCISES

In your opinion, does AAC seem like an intuitive fit for persons with ASD? Support your answer.

Write a brief description of a child or adult with ASD that uses AAC. Describe his or her system and note whether it is unaided or aided. Does the literature support the system or device choice made?

An affirmative answer to the first question in the exercise would reflect current thought. That is, the learning characteristics and preferences of persons with ASD (e.g., preferences for static as opposed to transient stimuli) seem to make AAC applications a logical intervention choice. If in the second question in the exercise you described an AAC option that was external to the user (e.g., symbol arrays, a VOCA), you described an aided system. If you mentioned support for gestures, signs, graphic symbols, or VOCAs, your answer was consistent with published literature.

Promoting Effective Practices

Guiding Principles

Ten guiding principles form the foundations of AAC service provisions over the course of the individual's life. Adherence to these principles promotes the likelihood of successful AAC services. This list is not exhaustive; it is a starting point from which providers can formulate and shape effective practices.

Early Intervention

Early intervention is critical to the success of AAC services. Characterizing factors include the following:

- Flexibility in early intervention enables creative responses to the ever-changing needs of children and families.
- Team commitment to evolving professional roles and responsibilities provides seamless service delivery.
- Recognition and response to diversity builds the cohesiveness necessary for effective practice.
- Family empowerment results in family ownership of and direction in services.
- An expanded interchange of information between professionals and families promotes optimal communication and collaboration.

Early intervention maximizes a child's development and reduces or alleviates the need for special services later in the child's life. Because the

The authors would like to acknowledge Stephen Von Tetzchner, Harold Martinsen, Pat Mirenda, David Beukelman, Lyle Lloyd, Carol Potter, Chris Whittaker, Jeanne Johnson, Dianne Baumgart, Edwin Helmstetter, Chris Curry, Regina Miller, Leslie Cochran, Mary Noonan, Dianne Bricker, Juliann Woods Cripe, Linda McCormick, Ruth Cook, Dale Carpenter, Diane Klein, and Annette Tessier for their assistance in formulating the principles addressed in this chapter.

17

early years are a crucial period in a child's development, the effects of principles established during this time can last throughout his or her life. The exchange between the child and his or her environment creates development. Tremendous growth occurs during early childhood, and failure at this time to address variables that interfere with development will subsequently affect the child's later development. Although untreated variables can have secondary disabling effects on the child, early intervention can help mitigate the occurrence of secondary disabilities.

Early intervention supports family needs, priorities, and resources. It differs from other support programs in that it melds participation of individuals from education, social services, and health sectors, all of which provide services that are vital to the well-being of families. Early services lessen the immediate impact of the disability on family function. Children receiving early intervention have more productive societal outcomes because it fosters less restrictive environments as the child passes through school. Early intervention has benefited families by instilling in them a more positive attitude toward the child's disability and encouraging them to seek greater support networks.

Individualization

The learning and development of skills varies among individuals and among the environments in which they interact. Individuals have different personalities and learning styles. It is obvious that individualization will affect AAC services in a variety of ways, ranging from symbol selection to system choices and multimodal system or device use.

All humans exhibit differences, the uniqueness of which defines us as individuals. These differences may be psychological or physiological, subtle or apparent. Whether differences equate to a disability may not be evident; however, any attention on an individual's disability should not limit recognition of his or her abilities. Although it is important to recognize disabilities for what they are, interactions with individuals with disabilities should focus on their abilities. Attending only to disabilities reduces one's ability to recognize the gifts and talents so often evident among persons with special needs.

Given the heterogeneity of the population of individuals and families to be served, no one set of interventions would be appropriate for all persons. Instead, individuals and families need to have plans, from assessment to intervention, specifically tailored to meet their unique needs.

Family Centeredness

Family-centered service delivery is a set of beliefs and practices that define particular ways of working with individuals and their families. They are consumer driven and competency enhancing. A family systems perspective is driven by core concepts including (a) a family system is more than the sum of its parts, (b) change in one part of the family system affects the whole system, (c) subsystems are embedded within the larger family system, (d) the family exists in a larger social or environmental context, and (e) family-centered care is multigenerational. AAC services must be family centered to truly be effective.

In a family-centered approach, families participate as decision makers and partners in planning and implementing programs and services. The family-centered approach provides opportunities to be involved in all aspects of programming, at the family's desired level of involvement. Interventions within a family-centered model not only enhance the skills and abilities of the individual but also allow families to identify their own concerns, priorities, and resources. The focus of service is to support and strengthen families as they address the needs of a family member with a disability.

A family-centered model acknowledges and fosters a diversity of tasks ascribed to family members as collaborators with professionals, including conducting assessments, prioritizing intervention goals, designing intervention plans, and implementing interventions. A requisite to employing a family-centered approach is understanding sources of both family diversity and culturally competent service provisions. Families represent a continuum of educational backgrounds, racial and ethnic backgrounds, and socioeconomic status. A family-centered practitioner is sensitive to these considerations. When family members are directly involved in planning and implementing services, family members become more knowledgeable and thus enhance their skills. They, in turn, become more effective in helping their family member with a disability achieve his or her maximum potential.

A family-centered approach builds on a family's identified strengths and abilities and provides opportunities for families to acquire knowledge, skills, and confidence. It creates opportunities for families to share concerns, priorities, and resources on an ongoing basis in ways that minimize disruptions to family life. These practices are centered on honesty and reciprocity.

Collaboration and Teaming

Collaboration involves the pursuit of a common goal through shared decision making. It requires equality among all parties. Collaboration is composed of a number of characteristics, some of which are easily met and others that pose significant barriers to family–professional relationships. These characteristics include (a) parity among participants, (b) voluntary participation, (c) identification of mutual goals, (d) shared responsibility in participation and decision making, and (e) shared accountability for outcomes. Collaborative processes are needed for AAC decision making to occur in accurate and socially valid ways.

Team processes have evolved as collaboration among professionals and families has increased. The transdisciplinary team model is the most collaborative of current team structures. It calls for team members to cross traditional disciplinary boundaries, asserting that both parents and professionals be involved in the assessment, planning, intervention, and monitoring of services, but that all members do not have to interact directly with the individual receiving services. The model emphasizes cross training in specialist areas with parents actively involved in different professional activities. There is a strong emphasis on parent participation with respect to planning and implementing program objectives. Arena-style assessments are encouraged, whereby parents and team specialists observe, consult, and periodically interact with the child within natural environments. Role release, consultation, integration of information, and team consensus are key factors in this approach. Transdisciplinary teaming is recommended in AAC service delivery.

The effectiveness of a team is linked to the collaborative skills of its members. A collaborative team has shared beliefs and interdependence specific to the skills, leadership, and abilities of all members.

Range of Approaches

A number of potential intervention strategies or approaches exist. Nowhere is this more evident than in training associated with the delivery of AAC services. The range of possible training options falls along a continuum of empirically validated strategies that include explicit (direct instruction and modeling) as well as implicit (individual initiated) methodologies.

Many of the explicit approaches include structuring routines, the social environment, and physical space. Explicit strategies may also include correspondence training, response shaping, peer-mediated training, and response prompting. Many of the more implicit approaches are centered on activity-based instruction or naturalistic strategies. These focus learning on child-initiated activities and embedding learning in routines. Implicit approaches also include embedding instruction in logically occurring antecedents and consequences (e.g., learning to climb so a child can go down a slide).

A major component of any approach is providing a high-quality learning environment, and designing instruction within a contingent or responsive environment is the first priority of effective instructional approaches. Contingent or responsive environments entail interactions in which individuals receive meaningful, consistent feedback about behaviors, especially those targeted in intervention efforts.

Good intervention approaches provide a balance of structured and spontaneously initiated learning. Whatever the approach used, the activity presented to the individual should be meaningful, balanced (as to the type of approach), and accessible to monitoring progress.

Social Validity

Social validity refers to the consequential basis of assessment or intervention. It addresses the needs and wants of society, the social appropriateness of interventions, and the acceptability and satisfaction of the recipients of the intervention. Social validity relates to the acceptability of test instruments and corresponding procedures, objectives and interventions, and the linkage of assessment practices, program planning, and evaluation. AAC services must be socially valid.

Central to the concept of social validity is the effect of the change on the direct consumer of the service, the indirect consumer significantly affected by the change, and the effect the change has on society at large. For the direct consumer, though, questions relating to how the service or proposed change affects personal satisfaction, individual empowerment, and happiness or enjoyment in life are all important concerns of social validity. The whole process of affecting change of another individual should be subject to questions throughout the individual's life.

Inclusion

Inclusion is characterized by being unnoticeable. It is not a concept that involves individuals being concealed or hidden—just the opposite. Inclusion is the fabric of our everyday lives. It is a concept that spans an individual's life. It is a commitment on the part of society to the idea that people belong together, not separated into individual groups, and that services should blend into individuals' environments rather than occur in isolated, discrete contexts.

During the school years, *inclusion* refers to the commitment to educate children with disabilities in the school and classroom they would not otherwise attend. Outside of school, and throughout an individual's life, it refers to societal institutions without boundaries that allow individuals to participate to the maximum extent possible in the community. AAC provides a participation bridge to increased inclusive opportunities for persons with severe expressive and receptive communication impairments.

The assumption underlying the concept of inclusion is equality. Treating individuals in a fair and equitable manner is inclusive. People more readily accept and care for others and become more accepting of individual differences in societies where inclusion is the norm.

Natural Environments

AAC assessment and implementation must occur in natural settings to be optimally effective. For any learning to be generative and lasting, skills need to be taught and practiced in the environments in which they are used. New skills need to be practiced in each of the environments in which an individual lives, goes to school, works, and plays. Teaching and learning skills in the individual's natural environment increases the likelihood that these skills will be logically reinforced. Learning occurs within the context of an individual's natural day.

It is inherently logical to teach and learn within the scheduled activities in an individual's day. Objectives can be addressed easily throughout the course of normal daily routines, which will allow the individual to anticipate necessary behaviors and learn through repetition.

By embedding learning in natural environments, one invariably introduces novelty into the teaching and learning cycle. Although structure and routines within a natural environment can facilitate learning, novel situations allow individuals to generalize what they have learned. Presenting an individual with opportunities to experience novel situations is an important component of learning within a natural context. The greatest advantage of natural environments is the ability to teach individuals to perform a task spontaneously at the appropriate time thereby increasing the likelihood of generalization of that skill.

Instruction within natural environments invariably involves naturalistic teaching approaches. These approaches make use of relatively brief interactions between individuals in low-structure settings and provide instruction based on an individual's focus of attention. Naturalistic teaching approaches share many characteristics, including (a) teaching that occurs in the natural environment, (b) teaching interactions that are brief and distributed over time, (c) instructional interactions that are typically initiated by the individual with disabilities, and (d) instruction that relies on natural consequences. Natural environments refer to all community settings, and activities that typically occur in these settings can reliably be conceived as natural activities.

Transition

In families that have a member with disabilities, transitions can be stressful events. The information, planning, support, and assistance individuals and families receive is critical to the transition's success. AAC services can create and provide solutions for life transitions.

General considerations for successful transitioning from infancy to adulthood have been developed, especially with respect to setting or program changes. First, family members should receive necessary information, support, and opportunities to enable them to participate as equal partners in transition planning. The family's goals for the transition are of primary importance, and families should receive assistance in obtaining information to achieve these goals. Second, planning transitions should occur in a systematic, individualized, timely, and collaborative fashion. A transition plan should be developed well in advance of the transition to the new environment, and the planning team should consist of parents and individuals from the present and future environments in which the individual will be involved. Third, the individual who is transitioning should be provided the opportunity to learn the appropriate skills that will promote successful participation in the new setting. Skills necessary for successful participation in the new setting should be identified early so they can be learned and practiced prior to the setting change. Fourth, the setting that is receiving the individual should prepare the environment for a successful transition. Receiving staff should obtain necessary training and technical assistance as well as the necessary resources, including personnel and equipment. Fifth, the transition planning team should determine strategies for promoting the individual's full participation in each situation and activity. And sixth, close monitoring of the transition and follow-up support for families is essential.

Life-Span Changes

AAC services must be responsive to life-span changes. Families change over time, and the individual with disabilities in a family goes through changes that affect not only him- or herself but other members of the family. Physical, emotional, and social changes in the individual with disabilities alter the priorities, resources, and needs of families.

The family also goes through life-cycle transitions. Parents growing older, siblings moving away, and worries about future care of the individual with disabilities all interact to enhance stress and strain on family units. Each family will bring different characteristics, styles, and values to address the stress of life changes. Each family's needs must be addressed on an individual basis, taking into account the level of support families may need to help ease the stress of change.

The family unit is an interactional system; what affects one member of the system can affect others. The interaction patterns of husband–wife, parent–child, and siblings can all elicit powerful emotions. When a child with a disability enters the family system, it may alter these interaction patterns. One cannot assume, however, that the impact would be negative.

Family units may go through a number of stages in reacting to a child with a disability including denial, bargaining, anger, depression, acceptance, or rejection. The manner in which families go through these stages, in terms of a time frame and ultimate resolution, will be affected by such things as culture, religion, coping styles, special problems, and family characteristics.

Over the course of time, it is hard to make generalizations about the effects of change on the family. Each life change may be a challenge for professionals and families. Change is a process most people resist. The numerous ecological and interactional variables that affect life-cycle change will be reflective of how families learn from and cope with transitions in life.

In summary, these principles permeate AAC services. Our responsiveness to them will, in large part, dictate how effective our efforts will be. The AAC story that follows in the next section highlights our practice principles across the life span of one individual.

Juan's AAC Story

J uan's story provides readers with an illustrative example of AAC applications across the life span. Though fictional, the story includes an aggregate of experiences typical of AAC intervention efforts with persons with ASD. Juan's case is described at five critical life intervals, including (1) identification to preschool; (2) preschool to early school age; (3) later school age; (4) high school to adult transition; and (5) adulthood. At each juncture, background history is provided, Juan's communication characteristics are described, and AAC interventions are reviewed. In addition, each life interval discussion includes exercises for the reader and a case interpretation specific to the authors' previously presented 10 principles for effective practice.

Identification to Early Intervention Period

Juan's early experiences are reviewed in this section. AAC interventions are discussed, and practice principles are considered.

History

Juan's story begins like that of many children with ASD. He was born to delighted parents and an adoring older sister. Juan's early medical and developmental history seemed unremarkable. By age 15 months, however, his parents recall Juan as being less interested in interaction than other children his age. He preferred to be alone, avoided eye contact, and demonstrated self-stimulatory behaviors (e.g., flapping, spinning, and repetitive manipulations of objects). Juan used a few words around his first birthday but regressed to gesture use by 15 months of age (e.g., Juan liked to lead others to things he wanted). During a routine medical exam at 18 months, Juan's mother expressed concern about her son. A discussion of Juan's development and behaviors led his pediatrician to order an evaluation by the local early intervention team. The team's case coordinator contacted Juan's family to review strengths and needs. In a preassessment staffing, the coordinator and Juan's parents decided they needed to know more about what might be causing Juan's behaviors and what could be done to help him develop. The case coordinator arranged for a transdisciplinary assessment to occur in Juan's home. With Juan's parents' input, she included the following discipline representatives in the assessment: a speech–language pathologist, a psychologist, an occupational therapist, and an early interventionist. The case coordinator informed Juan's parents of the team's desire for them to function as equal team members in the assessment. They discussed roles for Juan's parents during the assessment process (e.g., providing information, playing with Juan). Juan's assessment findings resulted in a diagnosis of ASD. He was reported to present developmental delays. Juan's communication was described as nonsymbolic (i.e., not a symbol user), and he was reported to have sensory issues specific to touch and feeding. Team findings also noted that Juan had difficulty with transitions within and between activities (e.g., completing a task and moving from one task to another). Juan was recommended for early intervention sessions three times weekly in his home. He participated in early intervention until he transitioned into an inclusive preschool setting at age 3. Juan received speech therapy and occupational therapy services throughout early intervention.

Communication Characteristics

The speech–language pathologist participating in Juan's initial evaluation described his communication as both nonsymbolic and primitive. Juan primarily communicated to request and protest, using gestures. Juan also protested using some behaviors such as head banging and biting (this occurred primarily during difficult transitions). His natural gestures exclusively involved contact with objects or people. He vocalized, but used few consonants and did not appear to use vocalizations intentionally. Juan's rate of communication was reported to be very low. It is interesting to note that Juan was reported to demonstrate some recognition of environmental symbols. For example, his mother said he became excited when he saw certain food labels (e.g., a favorite cereal box). Finally, Juan did not use eye gaze communicatively during interaction.

AAC Interventions

Initial early intervention efforts with Juan emphasized the promotion of natural gestures. The interventionist and Juan's parents worked together to create situations of high interest that would make gestures more likely (e.g., participating in turn-taking routines with favorite objects). As contact gestures began to occur more frequently, an effort was made to encourage distal gesturing (e.g., open palm requesting). This was met with limited success.

Juan's difficulty with activity transitions was addressed using an object–picture schedule for problem activities. For example, an object–picture array was created representing hair washing and dressing. The use of schedules appeared to help Juan develop expectations specific to his day.

Transition to early intervention services was facilitated by Juan's learning typical activities and creating picture schedules to use throughout the day. In early intervention, natural gestures continued to be promoted. In addition, Juan's speech–language pathologist, occupational therapist, teacher, and parents worked together to introduce simple signs representing general requests (e.g., "more" and "want"). Throughout early intervention programming, Juan's sign vocabulary grew at a slow rate to include signs for common objects and activities at home. By age 3, Juan used approximately 10 signs that were typically prompted by others (e.g., "Show me what you want—sign juice."). Near the end of his early intervention experience, Juan was introduced to the PECS system. He began to exchange line drawings to request objects and activities.

EXERCISE

Which of the 10 practice principles can you identify in Juan's case so far?

Practice Principles

Thus far, Juan's case illustrates at least five of our AAC practice principles. First, Juan was identified early. Current research suggests that early identification is critical if positive outcomes are to be attained for children with ASD (Wood & Wetherby, 2003). In Juan's case, early identification also led to early and positive family involvement.

The value of family-centered and team-based practices was also illustrated during Juan's early years. For example, Juan's pediatrician's attention to family concerns reflects a family-centered perspective. That is, she honors Juan's mother's concerns by recommending and arranging follow-up. Involvement of the early intervention team in Juan's assessment and its transdisciplinary functioning and family involvement also represent recommended practices.

That assessment and early intervention occurred in Juan's home demonstrates the use of natural settings. Too often, services are provided in clinical or educational environments due to long-standing policies and practices or provider convenience. In all probability, children like Juan will act most typically in their home. As a result, service providers can experience optimal success with assessment and intervention in that environment.

Finally, this segment of Juan's case highlights life-span changes. As Juan's family learns of his diagnosis and subsequent treatment needs, parental expectations will probably be adjusted. For example, anticipation of first words may change to hopes for increased unaided communication (i.e., gestures and signs). Of course, Juan experiences life-span changes at a personal level, including development and growth as well as his movement from one intervention program to another.

EXERCISE

Why do you think providers tried the PECS program with Juan? Was it a next logical step based upon the review in the Overview of AAC and ASD section of this manual?

PECS was a good choice for Juan at this early stage of his AAC story. He had experienced some success with nonsymbolic communication and had begun to use signs, although he needed prompting. Juan was also showing some recognition of two-dimensional graphic symbols (e.g., product labels). Furthermore, PECS may serve as a bridge to more independent initiations and flexible symbol use for children like Juan, especially those who show some predisposition for recognizing and using graphic symbols.

Preschool to Third Grade

Transition to the early school years can be difficult for all children. Here, Juan's early school years are described, his AAC interventions are discussed, and practice principles are applied.

History

The transition from infant and toddler programs to school-based preschool programs can be stressful for families. For Juan's family, leaving behind the therapists and teachers they came to know and trust was difficult. In the first years of Juan's life, the local mental health agency was the lead provider of services. Now, for the remainder of Juan's schooling, the local schools would be the provider of all services. Teams from both agencies met 6 months prior to Juan's transition into the local public preschool program. This first transition team meeting consisted of Juan and his parents, administrators, teachers, and therapists from both agencies. Meeting early in the transition process showed foresight by both groups. There were a few concerns, however, that Juan's parents discussed with the early intervention team after the meeting. Foremost, they observed that while Juan happily moved between early intervention personnel at the meeting, the school team seemed less interested in Juan. They seemed overly concerned with the process of moving Juan to the preschool, the amount of services he was presently receiving, whether the school would be able to afford to continue the same amount of services, and the need to have Juan do more assessments with the school-based personnel. Juan's parents were surprised at how differently the two systems operated. At no time did the school team ask the family if they had any needs or concerns; rather, they focused exclusively on Juan's needs. There were positive developments that came from the meeting, though. Juan would be placed in a regular preschool in his neighborhood with a teacher who had taught children with needs similar to Juan's. Although the special education director appeared formal (suit and tie), he seemed concerned about what was best for Juan. The speech–language pathologists from both teams knew each other and were eager to work together for Juan's benefit.

The transition went smoothly as Juan learned the survival skills he would need in preschool from his early intervention teacher. She observed these skills (primarily related to the need to communicate with peers) during a visit to his new classroom. Also, Juan spent a number of short sessions in the preschool with the teacher and classmates before he started full time. The 2 years in preschool generally went well for Juan. Testing confirmed ASD with mild mental retardation. Juan stayed with the same teacher for both years, lessening changes in routines. The preschool teacher used a play-based curriculum, affording Juan opportunities for interaction with his classmates. Juan's preschool teacher also noted that Juan learned best when she provided a model and then used different prompting strategies to engage Juan in the learning task.

The transition to the elementary school (kindergarten) did not go as well as the initial transition to preschool. Juan's parents felt they had little say during the meeting and that most of the conversation was between professionals, some of whom had never met Juan. They seemed to have a hard time agreeing on what was best for Juan and seemed focused on their own disciplines. This transition was difficult for Juan. He visited the classroom in the elementary school only once before school started and that was in the summer when neither the teacher nor students were present. When he began school in the fall, certain excess behaviors began to increase. It was hard to get him to board the bus, and he screamed and threw tantrums at school. Transitions between activities were particularly difficult for Juan. The teacher was becoming increasingly frustrated at her inability to communicate with him. She did not know his signs, could not interpret his communicative behavior, and did not have time to provide the one-on-one assistance Juan needed. A team meeting was called (Juan's parents could not attend because of work) and two main decisions were made: (a) a functional behavior assessment (FBA) would be completed to identify what may be influencing Juan's excess behavior, and (b) an individual aide would be provided for Juan at school.

For the next few years Juan remained in a general class setting with the same aide. The FBA provided useful information on the antecedents to Juan's behavior and the types of responses from people that may have reinforced problem behavior. Suggestions from the FBA focused on the importance of communicating transitions and consistency in addressing the behaviors that interfered with Juan's learning.

Although Juan was unable to keep up with his peers academically, he was provided an individual program in his classroom. Juan's special education teacher, who provided consultative services, felt that Juan could participate more in general class activities. His teachers, however, were inclined to have Juan's aide work with him at a back table. The learning came predominantly through explicit teaching strategies, focusing primarily on functional academic skills.

As Juan entered third grade, the team felt he should be pulled out of the general class a few hours a week for intensive language instruction. Although Juan's parents attended this meeting and expressed concern about Juan leaving his general classroom, the professionals at the meeting convinced them it was in Juan's best interest.

Communicative Characteristics

"All behavior is communication" best typifies Juan's communication during this period. Juan's excess behavior occurs when those in his environment are unable to accurately interpret his communication needs. Frustration on Juan's part is increased by the inability of children and adults to communicate with him through signs. By the third grade he is only occasionally signing at home and never in school. Although Juan continues to use non-symbolic gestures, he is becoming more of an emergent communicator using echolalia as a clear expressive form. Most of Juan's echolalic responses are generated from movies he has seen and are initially associated with times of stress or anxiety. Phrases such as "look out, look out," "it's all right little fella," or "come back" are always expressed at anxious moments and are from movies that portray stress or anxiety. Juan also uses echolalia to elicit responses from others. The words "elephant, elephant" are said with the expectation that the receiver will provide an exclamatory response, such as, "Oh no, the elephants are coming." This use of a favorite movie phrase sends Juan into fits of laughter.

The FBA notes the importance of Juan having a communication system to express his wants and needs. It is determined that given more sophisticated symbolic arrays, Juan is able to initiate more complex reciprocal communication than simply exchanging a symbol for an object. More sophisticated systems allow Juan to make choices, inquire about future events, and communicate using more abstract concepts (e.g., prepositions).

AAC Interventions

During his early elementary years, Juan moves from simple picture arrays and a picture exchange system (PECS) to increasingly large arrays of picture communication symbols (PCS). The PCS consist of 3,000 simple black-and-white line drawings on cards that depict nouns (e.g., *glass*), verbs (e.g., actions, such as *eat*), as well as cards printed with articles and prepositions. He is also introduced to voice output communication aids (VOCA) during his early school years. Initially, his use of VOCAs is environmentally specific. They are, for instance, used at a particular station during center-based time in preschool.

EXERCISE

Which of the 10 principles can you identify during the preschool to third grade period in Juan's life?

Practice Principles

During this time a number of principles have been illustrated, and you may identify more than are discussed here. Transition principles were noted on several occasions. Some best practices were noted during the first transition when team members met 6 months prior to Juan's transition, specific survival skills were taught before he entered the new environment, and multiple visits to the preschool were made before actually attending. Poor transitioning practices were noted in that only one visit to his new kindergarten occurred (without the teacher or students). You will probably note many more examples of poor transition practices. Differences in teaming styles were evident between the infant–toddler team and school-based team. Specifically, the infant–toddler team was transdisciplinary and the school-based team focused primarily on individual discipline perspectives.

A variety of instructional approaches were discussed, ranging from implicit (activity-based activities) to explicit (direct instruction and modeling) strategies. Also, inclusionary principles were particularly evident in Juan's preschool years, in which the teacher made efforts to include Juan in all class activities. Although Juan remained in inclusionary settings

31

throughout his early elementary years, he was increasingly excluded from many classroom activities and worked by himself at a table in the back of the classroom.

EXERCISE

What is the rationale for AAC use to help with issues associated with excess behavior?

If we realize that "all behavior is communication" and that behavior occurs generally because a child wants to get something (e.g., attention, object, explanation) or get away from something (e.g., task too difficult, pain), then we begin to realize how important it is to provide means for a child to communicate his wants and needs.

The Later School-Age Period

Juan's later school experiences are reviewed in the following section. In addition, his AAC interventions are discussed and practice principles are considered.

History

Soon after Juan's 10th birthday, his family relocated to accommodate a promotion for his father. The move was difficult for the family. Juan's sister was entering high school and found making friends a challenge. Her close relationship with Juan eased the stress of moving. Juan's parents were consumed with learning the new community and identifying resources that might help with Juan's care. His new school was supportive and tried to promote a smooth transition by contacting previous teachers about classroom objectives and supports. Juan was placed in a segregated classroom for students with mental retardation and autism. His academic work became increasingly functional. Juan was now capable of recognizing some simple print.

In the years that followed, Juan's family adjusted to their new community. Juan continued in self-contained placements with inclusive opportunities during school-wide activities. His teachers noted that Juan was often socially isolated. Specifically, he had few friends and his limited ability to initiate communication made engaging others difficult. Juan continued to demonstrate excess behaviors when frustrated or agitated. For example, he hit himself and others when daily routines were interrupted or in settings where high levels of stimulation occurred (e.g., very noisy environments).

Communication Characteristics

Throughout this period, Juan continues to communicate through unaided and simple aided AAC. In addition, his use of echolalia continues to grow. Juan now clearly uses immediate and delayed echo to request and protest. He also uses mitigated echo, illustrating a move to more generative speech. By age 14, Juan periodically uses short spontaneous utterances. These typically occur when he is prompted or engaged by partners. For example, to "How are you Juan?," he responds "Good today."

Juan's behavior becomes a significant problem, especially as community transitions are considered. A FAB reveals that behavior typically occurs when Juan wants to protest or escape undesirable activities. Juan's large size at age 14 makes his behavior a particular concern for family, teachers, and peers.

AAC Interventions

Many of the AAC interventions introduced during Juan's early school grades continue to be in place. In addition to echolalia and spontaneous speech, he now communicates with gestures, through very few limited signs (only at home), and with a simple VOCA (PCS symbol arrays with print). Most of Juan's spontaneous communication attempts involve gestures with contact and echolalia. Other communicative forms are prompted by his partners. Juan's VOCA is initially used in predictable settings in which communicative partners are likely to be unfamiliar (e.g., community outings with his class). VOCA use is being expanded in an attempt to increase Juan's success with initiating interaction. For example, PCS symbols expressing popular greetings and humorous sayings are being included in Juan's symbol arrays. In addition, Juan is participating in training to help him recognize opportunities to use these new symbols. Juan's partners are also using his VOCA to augment their communicative input. That is, as they provide choices or make requests of Juan, they select supportive symbols from his VOCA's symbol arrays.

Augmented input continues to occur through the use of picture schedules (PSC symbols with print) that represent Juan's daily activities. These schedules are used at home and in school to create predictability and expectancy for Juan. Juan's schedules have significantly helped with his behavior. There has also been a concerted effort to modify Juan's behavior through the use of a "stop" symbol. Because Juan's behavior is now primarily serving protest and escape functions, those around him have been encouraged to prompt Juan's use of a small stop sign at the first indication of behavioral outbursts. The symbol is red with an octagonal shape with the word *stop* printed across the sign. If Juan presents the stop symbol, he is allowed to change settings to calm down.

33

Finally, over the past few years, Juan has been introduced to computer-assisted instruction. He spends some time each day using classroom computers to help develop simple academic abilities (e.g., reading and writing). Juan enjoys the computer and is willing to do less exciting jobs to have increased computer time.

EXERCISE

Which of the 10 practice principles can you identify in this segment of Juan's AAC story?

Practice Principles

This span of Juan's story clearly illustrates three of our AAC practice principles. First, Juan's history reveals that he is frequently socially isolated and lacks meaningful peer interactions. At least two variables may be contributing to this problem: Juan's lack of communicative effectiveness and his frequent use of behavior. These problems were identified and incorporated into Juan's AAC intervention (e.g., VOCA use for initiations, schedules, use of the "stop" symbol). The decision by Juan's providers to implement these interventions is an example of selecting socially valid AAC goals. Socially valid intervention in this case is a clear example of selecting goals that were meaningful to Juan's future.

A second principle illustrated in this example is the effect of life-span changes on families and AAC services. The move of Juan's family required personal and professional adjustments that, in all probability, were stressful. In addition, Juan's progression from grade school to middle school brought new areas of focus (i.e., functional academics) and plans for the future (i.e., transition planning). Clearly, Juan's AAC services had to adapt to meet life-span issues. New environments called for new collaborative partners in the AAC process and new symbol choices. The shift in educational placement (i.e., inclusive to self-contained) resulted in different instructional goals, outcomes, and AAC applications.

Third, Juan's life-span changes brought forced and natural transitions. The family's move necessitated a school change. His educational needs resulted in a more restrictive school placement. The transitional planning in his Individualized Education Program (IEP) process brought new outcome objectives (e.g., job and community placement success). AAC services were affected by each of these transitions. Juan's new teachers worked to incorporate AAC interventions initiated by his former school. They built upon his existing systems by adding new VOCA applications, a behavior replacement strategy, and eventually computer-assisted instruction. Juan's placement in self-contained classes and emphasis upon transition to adulthood resulted in different activities, peers, and goals. These changes likely affected multiple aspects of AAC services including vocabulary choices, partners, and the implementation of augmented input and output strategies.

EXERCISE

How does Juan's addition of computer assisted instruction help deal with functional academics?

Juan's success with functional academics will improve his eventual chances for community life and work; however, children like Juan may not respond well to traditional academic instruction. This can relate to, among other things, attentional issues and sensorimotor deficits (e.g., hypo- or hypersensitivities and motor planning problems). Juan's interest in the computer and the availability of instructional software makes computer assisted instruction a logical choice.

High School to Adult Transition

For many adults with disabilities, the transition to adulthood can be difficult. Here, Juan's postschool life, AAC interventions, and practice principles are described.

History

The high school to adult transition was characterized by many changes for Juan. The biggest change was that his older sister moved away. Mary was his closest friend and was able to understand Juan's communicative behaviors better than anyone. She left at a time when Juan was transitioning to a new school and to a new program. It was also a time when there seemed to be more stress between his parents at home. During the initial phase of all these changes, Juan regressed both academically and behaviorally.

Juan's parents were increasingly concerned about how his life would be once his schooling was completed. They worried about whether he would have the skills, academically and socially, to live away from home. Although they could continue to care for their son, they began to realize that at some point, because of illness or death, they would not be able to meet his needs.

For the last few years, Juan had ostensibly been placed in self-contained settings, away from his age and grade peers. This would continue until he left school after age 21. At the end of eighth grade, when

Juan turned 14 years old, an important team meeting was held to map out issues related to Juan transitioning from school to work. Both Juan and his parents were involved in this meeting. Although his parents had had limited involvement in school decisions regarding Juan for many years, they were active and vocal participants at this meeting. Juan also actively participated by answering questions about likes and dislikes regarding a range of leisure and work-related activities. The team decided that Juan should transition the following fall into an occupational course of study.

During his ninth-grade year, Juan remained in school working on functional academics and job-related skills. Juan began exploring different work environments beginning in his 10th-grade year. Each day was different. He spent parts of days at WalMart, the local florist, a family friend's hardware store, and a local volunteer organization. Other days Juan's class visited banks or grocery stores to practice skills learned in the classroom. Spending time in the environments in which he would eventually work and live was helpful to Juan; however, the lack of a daily routine and consistent schedule had a negative effect on Juan's behavior.

With his sister's departure, his parent's increasing arguments at home, and the unpredictability of his days, Juan began to have serious and sometimes violent outbursts at school and in the community. Sometimes the outbursts seemed related to a particular event, but at other times they seemed to occur out of the blue. Because of his size and the nature of the outbursts, it was determined that another FBA was needed. The results of the assessment were not conclusive. It was clear from the FBA that at times certain antecedents in the environment and consequent reactions of adults were affecting the severity and occurrence of the excess behavior. At other times, no apparent causal factors appeared to precipitate the outbursts.

What was clear from the results was that changes in daily routines were having a profound effect on Jaun's behavior. Additional schedules were added to his workplace environments as well as a comprehensive weekly schedule. Also, the number of out-of-school visits were drastically decreased, then increased gradually over the next few years. His behavior improved immediately. He still had what appeared to be unrelated outbursts on occasion, but these became less frequent over the course of his remaining years in school.

When Juan was a senior and his classmates were graduating, his parents decided that he should remain in school through his 21st birthday and continue with the occupational course of study. Over the next 3 years, Juan came to spend a greater portion of his day in work-related settings. He also became more independent in his daily living skills. Through modeling, guided practice, and the use of graphic symbols, Juan was able to take the short bus ride from school to some of his workplaces. His teachers began incorporating more novelty into his daily routine. This was initially done by infusing a highly reinforcing activity in lieu of what was indicated on his schedule. The use of reinforcing activities was eventually faded to more everyday activities. Because of the gradual nature of these changes, Juan participated without incident.

Toward the end of Juan's schooling, he began to spend leisure time at a group home where some of his co-workers lived. Team members thought these positive experiences might help ease a transition to this home where he may eventually live.

Communication Characteristics

Use of schedules at home, work, and school continue to be an important component to easing transitions in Juan's life. He has become increasingly adept at using PCS and has also begun to use writing in communication. Juan initially paired PCS with the written word, copied the written word, and matched the word with the symbol. He was eventually able to communicate through the writing of about 50 words. During this period, Juan relies on both unaided and aided communication.

AAC Interventions

PCS arrays continue to be Juan's primary means of communication. Juan has devised his own system of organization and classification for the use of his symbols. He uses a portable 9 × 12 in. plastic box with dividers inside to help him organize his symbols. All the symbols and the top of the plastic container were fitted with Velcro strips, making the communication process easier for Juan.

Juan increasingly uses his VOCA in a variety of situations. The quality of the digitized speech and ease of VOCA use has made it an increasingly frequent communication choice. Additional VOCA use will be explored in the years to come.

EXERCISE

Which of the 10 principles can you identify during the 14- to 21-year period of Juan's life?

Practice Principles

The first principle considered was the team meeting that examined Juan's transition from school to work. The meeting was carried out at the appropriate time, when Juan turned 14 years old. Juan and his parents were active participants in the meeting. Next, life-span changes were noted by the departure of Juan's sister and the increasing anxiety of Juan's parents over their son's future. Social validity issues were then addressed by the types of programs in which Juan was involved, and the goals developed for Juan were deemed important for him and society. Finally, Juan's education increasingly took place in natural settings or environments in which he would eventually live and work.

EXERCISE

How has AAC aided in making the transition to the work place potentially more successful?

Juan's use of schedules at work helped organize his activities. His use of a portable PCS with symbols specific to his work environment increased the probability of communicative interaction and his ability to control his behavior through effective communication. In addition, the use of a more sophisticated VOCA system allowed supervisors and co-workers to more easily participate in reciprocal communication.

Adulthood

Adulthood presents challenges for us all. The scenario concludes with a discussion of Juan's adult experiences. AAC interventions are reviewed, and practice principles are considered.

History

After school, Juan lived with his parents for a few years and then moved into a community group home in his town. He resides with four other young men with autism. One year after Juan's move, his mother died somewhat unexpectedly. During a difficult period of adjustment, Juan's behavior escalated and he experienced some skill regression. Juan's sister moved back to his community to be more involved in his care. She visits Juan several times per week and enjoys taking him to eat and shop.

Juan works in a semicompetitive environment at a local hardware store owned by family friends. He spends 3 hours per day in the store stocking shelves and doing some simple inventory entry in the store's computer (Juan counts the number of stock items and enters data by the item name).

Juan is assisted in the store by the owner and a job coach from vocational rehabilitation (visits weekly).

Juan also participates in community outings sponsored by the county Association for Retarded Citizens (ARC). These events occur with others from the community and have been the source of positive social opportunities. For example, Juan has developed friendships with several ARC participants including Linda, his girlfriend.

Over time, Juan's father became ill and needed to be placed in a long-term care facility. His sister tried to become more involved in Juan's life in the absence of her parents. She began long-term care planning for Juan. Juan's behavior continues to be somewhat problematic. He experiences difficult periods associated with breaks in routines and sensory overload.

Communication Characteristics

Juan continues to use echolalia and limited spontaneous speech to communicate. In addition, he uses gestures and, when prompted, a multilevel VOCA.

AAC Interventions

Juan is now using a three-level (essentially three pages of symbols) VOCA with 20 PCS symbols and printed messages. Juan is capable of initiating some interactions with his VOCA. For example, he enjoys greeting others and telling jokes programmed into his device. These behaviors are particularly apparent during his social outings with the local ARC. Recently, the speech–language pathologist serving Juan's group home initiated the SAL program with Juan to augment language input and output. Juan's sister, boss, and ARC workers have all been involved in SAL training. Within 2 months, Juan increased the number of symbols he recognized and used and was communicating with his VOCA more frequently. Juan's spontaneous verbalizations increased during SAL training.

Juan has schedules with PCS symbols representing events associated with work and group home activities. His interactive partners use Juan's schedules in all settings. In addition, Juan continues to use a "stop" symbol to replace escape behaviors associated with frustration and overstimulating environments.

EXERCISE

What AAC practice principles are evident in this final section of Juan's story?

Practice Principles

Several practice principles are illustrated in this last segment of Juan's story. Once again, life-span issues affect Juan and his family. His mother's death, father's move to residential care, and sister's return to his community all illustrate life events that can have an impact on family functioning and AAC applications. Given the changes mentioned, Juan's sister clearly decides both to take the lead in his life planning and become more involved in Juan's daily activities (e.g., outings, SAL programming). Juan's sister appears poised to be a significant influence in his future.

As mentioned earlier in Juan's case, life-span changes bring transitions. Juan's move to adulthood results in a new residence, a community job, and new friends. He also becomes involved with a girlfriend through the ARC. These natural life transitions affect AAC decision making. New settings and friends bring new symbols and partners for communication and additional opportunities for transition schedules. Juan's life transitions also brings new opportunities for community involvement and an increased need to augment his input and output. The move to SAL training is a direct response to Juan's growing opportunities and needs.

This segment of Juan's life also represents the application of multiple approaches in service delivery. Thus far in Juan's case, little has been made of the many and varied approaches used to promote communication. In truth, at each stage of Juan's life, service providers, family members, and peers have used a variety of systems and approaches to facilitate his communicative competence. This point is illustrated in Juan's adulthood by partners' acceptance and encouragement of unaided and aided communicative means (e.g., speech, gestures, picture symbols, and VOCA use [SAL]).

A final principle illustrated in Juan's adult AAC use is the value of natural settings. Juan's growth and development has increased his involvement and communicative success in community activities. Teaching new skills in the setting where they are used is both intuitive and recommended practice. Therefore, it isn't surprising that Juan has experienced communicative growth since SAL training was initiated across multiple trainers and in multiple natural settings.

EXERCISE

How have AAC interventions made Juan's eventual success in the workplace and community more likely?

The success of Juan's community involvement (i.e., life and work) will be directly related to his ability to communicate effectively and to the reduction of his communicative behaviors. Juan's interventionists have chosen to address these issues directly by increasing his VOCA use to promote initiations and promoting behavior replacement strategies. If these efforts are successful, the likelihood of community success for Juan will rise significantly.

The situation involving Juan is a representative example of the AAC services provided to individuals with ASD and their families. Obviously, professionals and family members will be challenged as they work collaboratively to help individuals like Juan meet their potential through AAC. It is our hope that this manual has been and can continue to be a resource that makes each AAC journey less intimidating and more successful.

References

Adamson, L., Romski, M. A., Deffebach, K., & Sevcik, R. (1992). Symbol vocabulary and the focus of conversations: Augmenting language development for youth with mental retardation. *Journal of Speech and Hearing Research, 35,* 1333–1343.

Baltaxe, C., & Simmons, J. (1977). Bedtime soliloquies and linguistic competence in autism. *Journal of Speech and Hearing Disorders, 42,* 376–393.

Beukelman, D., & Ansel, B. (1995). Research priorities in augmentative and alternative communication. *Augmentative and Alternative Communication, 11,* 131–134.

Beukelman, D., & Mirenda, P. (1998). *Augmentative and alternative communication: Management of severe communication disorders in children and adults* (2nd ed.). Baltimore: Brookes.

Bloom, L., & Lahey, M. (1978). *Language development and language disorders.* New York: Wiley.

Bondy, A., & Frost, L. (1993). Mands across the water: A report on the application of the picture-exchange communication system in Peru. *The Behavior Analyst, 16,* 123–128.

Brook, S. L., & Bowler, D. M. (1992). Autism by another name? Semantic and pragmatic impairments in children. *Journal of Autism and Developmental Disabilities, 22,* 61–82.

Bryen, D., & Joyce, D. (1985). Language intervention with the severely handicapped: A decade of research. *Journal of Special Education, 19,* 7–39.

Buitelaar, J. K., van Engeland, H., de Kogel, K. H., de Vries, H., & van Hooff, J. A. (1991). Differences in the structure of social behavior of autistic children and non-autistic retarded controls. *Journal of Child Psychology and Child Psychiatry, 32,* 995–1015.

Carr, E., & Dores, P. (1981). Patterns of language acquisition following simultaneous communication with autistic children. *Analysis and Intervention in Developmental Disabilities, 1,* 1–15.

Carr, E., & Durand, V. M. (1985). Reducing behavior problems through functional communication training. *Journal of Applied Behavior Analysis, 18,* 111–126.

Clarke, S., Remington, B., & Light, P. (1988). The role of referential speech in sign learning by mentally retarded children: A comparison of total communication and sign-alone training. *Journal of Applied Behavior Analysis, 19,* 231–239.

Cobrinik, L. (1974). Unusual reading ability in severely disturbed children. *Journal of Autism and Childhood Schizophrenia, 4,* 163–175.

Cobrinik, L. (1982). The performance of hyperlexic children on an incomplete words task. *Neuropsychologia, 20,* 569–577.

Costello, J., & Shane, H. (1994, November). *Augmentative communication assessment and the feature matching process.* Miniseminar presented at the annual convention of the American Speech-Language-Hearing Association, New Orleans.

Dalton Moffitt, B. (1999). Assistive technology. In B. T. Ogletree, M. A. Fischer, & J. B. Schulz (Eds.), *Bridging the family-professional gap: Facilitating interdisciplinary services for children with disabilities* (pp. 152–163). Springfield, MO: Thomas.

43

Doss, S. L., & Reichle, J. (1991). Replacing excess behavior with an initial communicative repertoire. In J. Reichle, J. York, & J. Sigafoos (Eds.), *Implementing augmentative and alternative communication: Strategies for learners with severe disabilities* (pp. 193–215). Baltimore: Brookes.

Durand, V. M., & Carr, E. (1987). Social influences on "self stimulatory" behavior: Analysis and a treatment application. *Journal of Applied Behavior Analysis, 20,* 119–132.

Fay, W. (1969). On the basis of echolalia. *Journal of Communication Disorders, 2,* 38–49.

Frost, L. & Bondy, A. (2002). *The Picture Exchange Communication System.* Newark, DE: Pyramid Education.

Fulwiler, R., & Fouts, R. (1976). Acquisition of American sign language by a noncommunicating autistic child. *Journal of Autism and Childhood Schizophrenia, 6,* 43–51.

Glennen, S. (1997). Augmentative and alternative communication assessment strategies. In S. Glennen & D. DeCoste (Eds.), *The handbook of augmentative and alternative communication* (pp. 149–192). San Diego, CA: Singular.

Glennen, S., & DeCoste, D. (1997). *The handbook of augmentative and alternative communication* (pp. 149–192). San Diego, CA: Singular.

Goossens, C. (1989). Aided communication intervention before assessment: A case study of a child with cerebral palsy. *Augmentative and Alternative Communication, 5*(1), 14–26.

Hodgdon, L. (1995). Solving social-behavioral problems through the use of visually supported communication. In K. Quill (Ed.), *Teaching children with autism: Strategies to enhance communication and socialization* (pp. 265–286). New York: Delmar.

Howlin, P. (1982). Echolalia and spontaneous phrase speech in autistic children. *Journal of Child Psychology and Psychiatry, 23,* 281–293.

Koegel, L. K. (1995). Communication and language intervention. In R. L. Koegel, & L. K. Koegel (Eds.), *Teaching children with autism: Strategies for initiating positive interactions and improving learning opportunities* (pp. 17–32). Baltimore: Brookes.

Lloyd, L., Fuller, D. R., & Arvidson, H. H. (1997). Introduction and overview. In L. Lloyd, D. R. Fuller, & H. H. Arvidson (Eds.), *Augmentative and alternative communication: A handbook of principles and practices* (pp. 1–17). Boston: Allyn & Bacon.

Lyon, S., & Lyon, G. (1980). Team functioning and staff development: A role release approach to providing educational services for severely handicapped students. *Journal of the Association for the Severely Handicapped, 5,* 250–263.

McLean, L. K., Brady, N. C., McLean, J. E., & Behrens, G. A. (1999). Communication forms and functions of children and adults with severe mental retardation in community and institutional settings. *Journal of Speech, Language, and Hearing Research, 42,* 231–240.

McCarthy, C. F., McLean, L. K., Miller, J. F., Paul-Brown, D., Romski, M. A., Rourk, J. D., & Yoder, D. E. (1998). *Communication supports checklist for programs serving individuals with severe disabilities.* Baltimore: Brookes.

Mirenda, P. (2001). Autism, augmentative communication, and assistive technology: What do we really know? *Focus on Autism and Other Developmental Disabilities, 16*(3), 141–151.

Mirenda, P., & Erickson, K. A. (2000). Augmentative communication and literacy. In A. M. Wetherby & B. M. Prizant (Eds.), *Autism spectrum disorders: A transactional developmental perspective* (pp. 333–368). Baltimore: Brookes.

Ogletree, B. T. (in press). The communicative context of autism. In R. Simpson & B. Myles (Eds.), *Educating children and youth with autism: Strategies for effective practice.* Austin, TX: PRO-ED.

Ogletree, B. T. (1999). Introduction to teaming. In B. T. Ogletree, M. A. Fischer, & J. B. Schulz (Eds.), *Bridging the family–professional gap: Facilitating interdisciplinary services for children with disabilities* (pp. 3–11). Springfield, MO: Thomas.

Quill, K. (Ed.). (1995). *Teaching children with autism: Strategies to enhance communication and socialization.* New York: Delmar.

Roberts, B. (1989). Echolalia and comprehension in autistic children. *Journal of Autism and Developmental Disorders, 19,* 271–282.

Romski, M. A., & Sevcik, R. (1996). *Breaking the speech barrier: Language development through augmented means.* Baltimore: Brookes.

Rutter, M., & Lockyer, L. (1967). A 5 to 15 year follow-up study of infantile psychosis. II: Social and behavioral outcomes. *British Journal of Psychiatry, 113,* 1183–1199.

Schepis, M. M., Reid, D. H., Fitzgerald, J. R., Faw, G. D., Van Den Pol, R. A., & Qelty, P. A. (1982). A program for increasing manual signing by autistic and profoundly retarded youth within the daily environment. *Journal of Applied Behavior Analysis, 15,* 363–379.

Schuler, A. (1995). Thinking in autism: Differences in learning and development. In K. A. Quill (Ed.), *Teaching children with autism: Strategies to enhance communication and socialization* (pp. 11–32). New York: Delmar.

Schuler, A., & Baldwin, M. (1981). Nonspeech communication in childhood autism. *Language, Speech, and Hearing Services in the Schools, 12,* 246–257.

Sheinkopf, I. S., Mundy, P., Oller, D. K., & Steffens, M. (2000). Vocal atypicalities of preverbal autistic children. *Journal of Autism and Developmental Disorders, 30,* 345–354.

Sigafoos, J., Drasgow, E., & Schlosser, R. W. (2003). Strategies for beginning communicators. In R. W. Schlosser (Ed.), *The efficacy of augmentative and alternative communication* (pp. 324–341). Boston: Academic Press.

Silberberg, N. E., & Silberberg, M. C. (1967). Hyperlexia: Specific word recognition skills in young children. *Exceptional Children, 34,* 41–42.

Stengel, E. (1964). Speech disorders and mental disorders. In A. U. S. de Reuck & M. O'Conner (Eds.), *Disorders of language* (pp. 285–287). Boston: Little, Brown.

Twachman-Cullen, D. (2000). More able children with autism spectrum disorders: Sociocommunicative challenges and guidelines for enhancing abilities. In A. M. Wetherby & B. M. Prizant (Eds.), *Autism spectrum disorder: A transactional developmental perspective* (pp. 225–250). Baltimore: Brookes.

Webster, C., McPherson, H., Sloman, L., Evans, M., & Kuchar, E. (1973). Communicating with an autistic boy by gestures. *Journal of Autism and Childhood Schizophrenia, 3,* 337–346.

Weitz, C., Dexter, M., & Moore, J. (1997). AAC and children with developmental disabilities. In S. Glennen & D. DeCoste (Eds.), *The handbook of augmentative and alternative communication* (pp. 395–444). San Diego, CA: Singular.

Wetherby, A. M. (1986). Ontogeny of communicative functions in autism. *Journal of Autism and Developmental Disorders, 16,* 295–316.

Wetherby, A. M., Prizant, B. M., & Hutchinson, T. (1998). Communicative, social-affective, and symbolic profiles of children with autism spectrum disorder. *American Journal of Speech-Language Pathology, 7,* 79–91.

Wetherby, A. M., Yonclas, D., & Bryan, A. (1989). Communicative profiles of children with handicaps: Implications for early identification. *Journal of Speech and Hearing Research, 54,* 148–159.

Wilcox, J. (1989). Delivering communication-based services to infants, toddlers, and their families: Approaches and models. *Topics in Language Disorders, 10,* 68–79.

Wood, J., & Wetherby, A. M. (2003). Early identification of and intervention for infants and toddlers who are at risk for autism spectrum disorders. *Language Speech and Hearing Services in Schools, 34,* 180–192.

About the Editor and Authors

Richard L. Simpson is a professor of special education at the University of Kansas. He currently directs several federally supported projects to prepare teachers and leadership professionals for careers with children and youth with autism spectrum disorders. Simpson has also worked as a teacher of students with disabilities, psychologist, and administrator of several programs for students with autism. He is the former editor of the professional journal *Focus on Autism and Other Developmental Disabilities* (published by PRO-ED) and the author of numerous books and articles on autism spectrum disorders.

Billy T. Ogletree is a professor in the communication sciences and disorders program at Western Carolina University. His research and clinical interests include the communication abilities and needs of persons with severe disabilities and autism. Related to these interests, Dr. Ogletree has written numerous articles and chapters on this subject and has been the recipient of federal grant funding to support personnel preparation efforts.

Thomas Oren is an associate professor of special education at Western Carolina University (WCU). He completed his graduate work at The Pennsylvania State University in special education and early childhood special education. He currently teaches in the birth–kindergarten program at WCU and teaches coursework in reading, classroom management, and student teacher supervision in the special education program. His interests include working with Full Spectrum Farms, a nonprofit organization dedicated to developing a farm community for adult persons with autism.